The Duet
An Anthology of Poems

Toki and Damola Mabogunje

AMV Publishing Services

Published by
AMV Publishing Services
23 Hampshire Drive
Plainsboro, NJ 08536
Tel(s): 6095770905 & 7326476721 Fax: 6097164770
africarus1@comcast.net & africarus@aol.com

The Duet An Anthology of Poems
Copyright © 2009 Toki and Damola Mabogunje

All rights reserved. No part of this publication may be reproduced, stored in a retrieval system, or transmitted in any form or by any means, electronic, mechanical, photocopying, recording or otherwise without the written permission of the Publisher.

Book Design: 'Damola Ifaturoti
Cover Design: Dapo Ojo-Ade

Library of Congress Control Number: 2008942860

ISBN: 0-9766941-1-5 (10-Digit)
        978-0-9766941-1-3 (13-Digit)

Contents

Introduction: Progression & Perspective.... *5*
Foreword by Prof. Femi Osofisan ... *7*
Life Is ... *9*
The Number 64 ... *11*
The Mother I Love So Much ... *13*
Untitled ... *14*
New Beginnings ... *15*
The World is Such a Beautiful Place ... *16*
The Future ... *17*
Striding Ahead ... *18*
Untitled ... *20*
Untitled ... *21*
Untitled ... *23*
My Sonnet: The Spoils of War ... *24*
My Dad ... *25*
See You at The Movies ... *26*
Christmas Day ... *27*
Serenity ... *28*
A Bright Light ... *30*
Abuse ... *31*
Consolidating The Vision ... *33*
Imagination: Foundation of the Nation ... *34*
Inspiration ... *36*
For The 1st Time ... *37*
An Easter Thought ... *38*
My 1st Limerick ... *39*
Injustice ... *40*
Niagara Falls ... *42*
Love's Cycle ... *44*
Tunnel of Babel or Babel in The Subway ... *46*
Life's Journey ... *48*
The Game Machine ... *50*

One Fine Day ... *52*
Despair ... *54*
Children at Play ... *55*
Desire ... *56*
Cookies and Cream ... *58*
Silence ... *60*
Divine Moments ... *62*
Crushed... *63*
Breathless ... *65*
Images ... *66*
What is WroOong with You!? ... *67*
The Value of a Life ... *69*
Mercy, why do you spare me? ... *71*

Introduction

Progression & Perspective

In going through this collection of poems, I see two things, Progression and Perspective. I read the poems I wrote back when I was eight and I laugh. It's quite nostalgic. I see how simple life was as an eight year old, I see how deeply insightful one can be when your mind hasn't started to get closed by growing up, I see myself going off in tangents of creativity. Then I read on, and see my poems in 2004, just 4 years ago (at age 16) and the difference is clear, topics are more defined, hardly any diversions, more profound subjects.... I see "progression", I see myself growing up.

Then I look at my mother's poems and see some of the same topics and I think to myself "You've still got a long way to go." At what point will I start looking at problems of the world and not just mine and those around me. At what point will I need to use words like "serenity" and "lethargic" to define the depth of my meaning? (I know them now, but they still seem too heavy to use). At what point will I be able to write about love in all its glory and despair? At what point will my perspective change?

At what point, will I be able to look back on my life and say.......

"I am well pleased." ('New Beginnings')

Adedamola Ifedayo Mabogunje

Foreword

On "THE DUET"
by
TOKI and DAMOLA MABOGUNJE

This anthology of poems will both startle, and delight. The first surprise will come from its uniqueness – it is the first time, as far as I am aware, at least in the history of modern Nigerian poetry, that a mother and her son would collaborate in such a joint venture of creativity. In this collection which they call a "duet", they have assembled their poems under a single title, instead of separating them into two distinct sections.

The effect therefore, as we proceed from poem to poem, moving from the voice of mother to that of the son and then back again and again, is like listening to a complex web of alternating strophes and antistrophes, witnessing the delicate process by which a long song constructs and deconstructs itself. There is always a tantalizing suggestion of travelling to and fro in time, between generations, that what we are reading is the profile of what the older poet used to be, or what the younger poet will grow to resemble.

The individual identities are not cancelled of course, since each poem is signed at the bottom, and the dates of composition supplied. But even without these signatures the attentive reader will still be able to distinguish between the younger poet's still inchoate yearnings and the unsteady touch – as evident for instance in his somewhat frantic straining for effects, in the crick and crack of forced rhymes and so on – and the mother's more mature, more confident handling of syntax and phoneme, her serene grace. Indeed serenity is the dominant mood of her poetry. Poem after poem reveal an inner calm, the mood of a spirit sheltered from turbulence ("The World is Such a Beautiful Place"), at peace with itself, ("New Beginnings"), and blessed with an irrepressively optimistic view of life ("The Future"). This is even more striking in that one reads the poems against the accompanying beat of her son's youthful and passionate gropings.

Both poets are of course still in the process of growth and (self-) discovery. Some poems here are in my view unnecessarily prolix and structurally slack. But all in all, I believe that this collection offers us a good "duet" that is for the most part pleasing to the ears.

Femi Osofisan
December 2008. Ibadan

LIFE IS

Life is what it will be
Life brings what it may
Life may be eternal
At work and at play
Life takes time
Time takes life

See while you are counting the seconds you live
Or planning the meetings
Or just being primitive
The seconds you are counting
Are counting on you

Not to waste or mind them
But to do what you do
But the seconds are also controlling what you do
If you dare to think about them
They think about you

Seconds are time
Time controls you
It tells you when to go somewhere
And tells you what to do

Life is what it will be
Life brings what it may
But if time controls it
Then what am I to say

The Duet An Anthology of Poems

The relationship of time and life
May turn a funny way
Because life controls time
And time controls life

Life is what it will be
Life brings what it may
If that's the way the world is
Then I have no say

© Damola Mabogunje
August 1999

THE NUMBER 64

64 is an even number
That's not all that's there
It's divisible by 2
And that's not new
So go and comb your hair

It also is a square
And some of them are rare
8 x 8 is the number
That is its pair

It is not odd
And that's no fraud
I hope that this is clear
Odd numbers have two factors
Extinction goes to raptors

64 is composite
This is not idiotic
That is why it's not a prime
And this poem has to rhyme

It's composite 'cause it has more than two factors
And as I've told you extinction goes to raptors
64 and 32
Common factors between them two
Common multiples are there too
And that should be all between them two

You don't know what a multiple is
Sort of like 64 x 2 to 8
L.C.M. is a common multiple
Just lower than the average common multiple
G.C.F. means greatest common factor
Unlike babies of a giant little raptor

This is my factor tree

64
2 x 32
  2 x 6
    2 x 3
2 x 2 x 2 x 3
23 x 3 = prime factorization
And that is the end of thee

© Damola Mabogunje
November 15th 1998

THE MOTHER I LOVE SO MUCH

My mother, my mother I love her so much
I love her dearly and that's a lot
She is the one who cooks my lunch
And washes and cleans the dirty spot

She buys me things here and there
Shows me that it's alright to care
When I make a stupid mistake
She shows me what is not at stake

This poem is dedicated to my mom
The one I love, the very best

THANK YOU MOM !!!!!!!!!!!!!!!!

© Damola Mabogunje
Class 601
Age 10

UNTITLED

Uncle Kolapo was a friend you couldn't beat
When it came to talk he was absolute
He was very relaxed
And very thoughtful
He bought us presents that he thought would be useful

When he decided to throw me up and down
I thought he would throw me right out of town
As you know he was my good godfather
There was nothing you could say, nothing you could do
To beat Uncle Kolapo out of his due

Like you Aunty Rosalie he was very kind
He may have driven you out of your mind
Without no foe
He had to go
It is part of the circle of life you know

There is nothing I can do
Nothing I can say
To bring Uncle Kolapo back to stay
This is all I can do my fine lady
I can cheer you up like no other baby

This is all that I have to say
I hope you like it
Good night and good day

© Damola Mabogunje
Untitled and written on the death
Of his godfather Kolapo Oyefeso
In 1999

NEW BEGINNINGS

There have been so many years of silence
The inner spirit unable to express itself
Was it the turmoil of human existence ?
A child born at age sixteen ?
The earlier loss of virgin state ?

Years have passed
Maturity has deepened
Here I stand now
Willing to be at peace with myself
And with all around me
I smile and I say
This is my life
The life I have chosen
And I am well pleased

© Toki Mabogunje
Friday 24th January 1997

THE WORLD IS SUCH A BEAUTIFUL PLACE

I look up and see the bright blue sky
The white fluffy clouds shimmering by
I see the sun's striking white light
On a typical hot African afternoon
What a sight !!!!!

Beads of sweat roll across my furrowed brow
As I wonder at the vibrancy of nature
On my continent Africa
This rapture
I feel now

Are we blessed or what ?
Humanity takes for granted
These things of nature
I lower my eyes
And follow the path of a butterfly
Across a rich green lawn
Over a bed of flowers

A worried thought cuts into my serenity
And I cast it aside impatiently
We must take the time to acknowledge
And to worship
Nature

© Toki Mabogunje
27th March 1997

THE FUTURE

The future is bright
The birds are singing
The sun is shining
Oh what a delight !

Out there on the horizon
Sits my life's goal
Pretty as a peacock
Preening its feathers

Playing hard to get
But I know
And so do you
That its only a matter of time
I bet ....

My arms outstretched
I shall grab you with both hands
And hold you aloft for all to see
Like a trophy you shall be
My trophy
My life's goal accomplished !!!!

© Toki Mabogunje
10th June 1997
Written for my sister Dudu

STRIDING AHEAD

What brought on this yearning?
This desire to find a life's purpose?
To improve on relationships
And to develop spiritually?

It was a dissatisfaction
The lack of progress
And communication problems
Within loves tie

I searched, researched
Read books from far and near
Then slowly but surely
A light began to shine
In the dark abyss

A ray of hope
Which as the days went by
Became the light of the sun
And the dawning of a new tomorrow

I looked back
And there he was
My only one
Keeping in step with me
Stretching, probing
Wanting to see
What I have seen

Toki & Damola Mabogunje

I drag him closer to me
I say look !!!!
Isn't it wonderful
And he says to me
With shutters closing over his eyes
Yes! It is !

His steps begin to falter
His movement more lethargic
His interest wanes
His eyes dart around
For some other distraction

I guess he has seen
All he wants to see
For now

He knows not that this
Ray of sunshine
Strikes a chord deep in my heart
Lifting me to a higher consciousness

Maybe one day he will look
Me in the eye
And see the wonders to behold
Then his step shall quicken
And we shall be side by side
Loving and supporting one another
As we strive for greater heights

© Toki Mabogunje
18th July 1997

UNTITLED

I may not know what to do or
Feel but I really have a need
To compose and expose are my daily feed

I hear these things and see these
Which I do not understand
But when I put them together they create
A great mirage
U can call it a façade or call it
What you may
But there is no difference no matter what
U say
Behind it there is nothing
And nothing it may stay

But it's the great circle of life
That keeps it on its way

© Damola Mabogunje
4th August 1999
Untitled

UNTITLED

You keep things here and keep them there
And to you they are safe nowhere
But if you think like a deer
You may say its safe anywhere
For if you trust no one
And no one trusts U
How are U to live
Without sleep or food ?
If you live like animals
You will understand
Trust and care
For they live in harmony
And know who to spare

The squirrels warn the rabbits
Who go to their burrows
The rabbit warns the mole
Who warns the giraffe
The giraffe warns the elephant
Who warns all the animals.
Why?

Because a man has walked
Into the forest
Because of one man
All the animals are scared
They know man is not to be trusted
Because of his weapons and armour
Man should be wasted
Man is the most untrusted
Being on the planet

And we have to change that
To be simple and kind
To be safe when we look behind

This is the way to live.

© Damola Mabogunje
4th August 1999
Untitled

UNTITLED

This government of ours
That is bad and distraught
Is leading us to be mad and corrupt

The titanic and its crew
Are a better way to explain
What will happen to the country
If we are kept on a chain

The majority of our country
Is really very poor
And all they are asking
Is for democracy to open its door

© Damola Mabogunje
10th August 1999
Untitled

MY SONNET

THE SPOILS OF WAR

The battle lingers on
Our brothers have been slain
The feeling here is pain
We're always on the run

We rise against our foe
With bullets from our guns
Like Caesar and the Huns
Contested long ago

The sorrow in our homes
Is the success of their plight
Why do we continue to fight ?
And turn our flesh to bones

There's nothing left anymore
These, are the **spoils of WAR**

© Damola Mabogunje

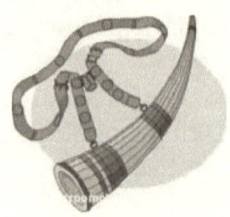

MY DAD

My Dad, My Dad
He works so hard
He comes home late
And lends a hand

He helps my mother
Then sleeps till dawn
And when he wakes up
It's after ONE !!!!

There's something that you ought to know
He's a very good father
He's not so so

And if you really have to know
To me he's great
I have to go

© Damola Mabogunje
Class 601

SEE YOU AT THE MOVIES

See you at the movies
On a very good night
See you at the movies
When the moon shines bright

© Damola Mabogunje
August 1999

CHRISTMAS DAY

Christmas day is coming soon
Gifts at stores are going to bloom
Mom and Dad play Father Christmas
While school is out on the day called Christmas

Actors go to act in plays
There are lots of good parades
In French, red is rouge
And they would also be showing Scrooge

My Dad will be coming on Christmas day
He'll buy a present
We'll shout HURRAYYYY!!!!!!!!!!!

© Damola Mabogunje

SERENITY

As I sit on the bare sand
At the beach
I look out over the great expanse
Of the ocean beyond my reach

The cool ocean breeze washes over me
I hear the loud beat of the
Ocean waves against the
Sandy shore

The branches of the coconut trees
In the woodland behind me
Wave and chatter
As they give way to the
Elements that matter

There is so much peace and
Serenity here
The sound of children's laughter
And the muted voices of
Adults in conversation
Gives vibrancy and life
To this sphere

The horizon
Draws that line between
The water and the sky
Yet it is not a barrier
To the great world beyond
Its mystery is in the fact

That it seems within your grasp
Yet it isn't
That is life's mystery
Isn't it ?

© Toki Mabogunje
24th August 1997
Coutonou, Republique du Benin

A BRIGHT LIGHT

A bright light shines ahead
Out there on the horizon
A strange white light
With a warm and loving glow

I know not what it signifies
Nor what message it brings
I do know its inviting glow
Beckons me where it leads

I shall set out on this adventure
I shall be well prepared
For any eventualities
Or any opportunities

An excitement wells up inside me
Oh what a trip of discovery
What is life without such risks
But a predictable uninteresting chore

I shall walk into that light
And basque in all its glory
I shall take what it has to offer
And turn it into a brand new story
I shall make history
With that light

© Toki Mabogunje
10th September 1997

ABUSE

Lord knows how many people
Have suffered some kind of abuse
The torridness of society
Is enough to make me obtuse

People turn a blind eye
To all the unkindness around them
We refuse to recognize
Or acknowledge
That dark side in us ....

Physical, sexual, child, wife
Or whatever the abuse
Does great damage
To the human psyche

We see various kinds of madness
Violence and other responses
To this form of human degradation
And we seem surprised
That these deviant forms exist

Wake up society
And face your ills
The only way to build
A better tomorrow
Is to consciously and collectively
Recognise and acknowledge
All forms of abuse
And commit ourselves
To resolving the problem

It is heartbreaking
To see the human suffering
Which attends
The victims of this
Socially deviant behaviour

Take heart dear ones
Have faith in the human spirit
Perhaps one day
Somewhere
A spiritual consciousness
Will arise
And the human spirit
Will soar once more

© Toki Mabogunje
10th September 1997

CONSOLIDATING THE VISION

Consolidating our vision
Is the number 1 mission
With God on our side
This vision is glorified

We boldly lead the way
Our goal shall never sway
Because the road is rough
We will have to be tough

Our conquest shall be known
When our vision has been grown
But now our cause is young
That's why we must be strong

We'll cross the raging sea
We'll make a legacy
We'll go as far as far
Atlantic Hall is who we are

© Damola Mabogunje
Winner Atlantic Hall Founder's
Day Poem

IMAGINATION
Foundation of the Nation

As my Dad talks and my Aunt showers
My Mother is sleeping and I have lots o' powers
One of them is, drawing, art
The others are musicality, poetry, an' craft
And if I may say imagination
Is the strongest of them all foundation of the nation
If you think of the days, long before now
These things that we have were dreams to be ploughed
The earth still looks flat
Although it is round
You can't fall off the earth
For there's gravity around

Things that we see
And things that we make
Put them together
And mix 'em and bake
And all of a sudden
A whole new idea
Popped into yer head
From out o' nowhere

Toki & Damola Mabogunje

The people from London, New Hampshire, Japan
The people who put the egg in the pan
The people from Australia, Africa, Asia
The people from Nigeria, Ghana and Malaysia
The people from the wars who aren't dead yet
The people who still can't buy a homeless dead pet
The people who come from all over the world
To see a fight fought over three little girls

There's nothing as boring as ever was yet
As when Nap. Bonaparte fell to his own death
There's still all those wars being fought out with such rage
That one in Iraq, that one in a cage
The one where the people are dying of old age

I must finish this poem to my own dismay
I have to go now, good night and good day

© Damola Mabogunje
January 30th 1999

INSPIRATION

Inspiration is for me
The Mom of creativity
The force that livens up the mind
For some of us it is undefined

It may be the atmosphere
A thing you like, or, something you fear
A love you lost, A love you found
Or just a thought, deep and logically sound

But when speaking professionally
Inspiration seems to lose its depth
For example, Biologically
Inspiration is a synonym for breath

For those of us who get inspired often
From time to time our hearts should soften
Look back on what inspired you
A person, place or thing you hate
A person, place or thing you love
Or perhaps someone you were jealous of

No matter what it may be
Or how you felt at the time
Try and remember it dearly
For therein lies the only sign
Of recognition and a lesson learnt

© Damola Mabogunje
1.00am 24th June 2004

FOR THE 1ST TIME

I have been here before
And 'twas not a dream
I've been round the airport
The town I have seen

The first time I came
I came unprepared
Yet I enjoyed all the treasures
And brewed what I feared

Now I re-visit
The place I have been
No more surprises
Prepared 4 anything

Still, coming to this place
So called "one and the same"
I start to realize is
A whole different ball-game

The problems are there
Some new and some gone
The treasures are the same
But somehow different ones

A new perspective
With the same stand point
Because
After the passage of time
Every re-visit
Is the 1st of its kind

© Damola Mabogunje

AN EASTER THOUGHT

On Easter Sunday, Monday and week
One must take the time to seek
And find out just what God has done
By giving us his only son

Who suffered and endured much pain
To make his killers righteous again
To cleanse us from all previous sin
Including crucifying him

Who descended to the depths of hell
To free those condemned to shout and yell
To stop the weeping and gnashing of teeth
And bring them up from down beneath

Who performed miracles and fed 5000
Who walked on water and on dry land
Who raised the dead and healed the sick
Who never sinned or played a trick

And on this day we must remember
The man who died for us to be
The God who gave to make us free
And though we still are such a mess
Remember J – E – S – U – S.

© Damola Mabogunje
28th March 2005

MY 1ST LIMERICK

A woman got off an xpress
And the door caught the hem of her dress
So when the train took off
Her dress tore off
And she was left naked and distressed

The dress ended up in Tuscany
Where a beggar put it in her trolley
For her it was good luck
She sold it 4 huge bucks
And bought herself a new Audi

Now isn't that story unlikely
And the narration uncanny
But if it were true
Say, what would you do
Wouldn't you wait 4 the express to Tuscany

© Damola Mabogunje
2nd May 2005

INJUSTICE

What must it be like
To have your freedom
Taken away from you

Political detainees
Human Rights Activists, Suspects
Precious human life
Treated with disdain

From whence comes
This feeling of superiority
This feeling of immortality
You are human too

Have you not realised
That in building this jungle of injustice
You trap yourself and thine own

What purpose does this serve
But the selfish interests
You think that by trapping
The lions in the forest
There lurks no danger still

Toki & Damola Mabogunje

Wake up, open your eyes
Look around you
Now that the lions are gone

Other animals shall discover
Their innate ability
To challenge that which
Poses a danger to society

In nature there must always be a balance
Something must give
Someplace, somewhere

© Toki Mabogunje
16th September 1997
Written on the death of Ken Saro-Wiwa

NIAGRA FALLS

The majestic splendor of nature's might
Captures the mind
When all around
The silence is broken
By the sound of crashing streams

The beauty of winter
Is all abound
In the frothy waters
Of Niagra Falls

The surrounding woods
Its floors covered
In ice and snow
The bare trees
Stark against the
Winter white

The calm feel
The serene scene
The peace
Its there for all to see

Toki & Damola Mabogunje

The smite of nature's
Powerful blow
Leaves not a pain or hollowness
But an all encompassing
Expansive love
And an awesome
Respect for creation

© Toki Mabogunje
3pm
29th December 1998
Niagra Falls
New York State

LOVE'S CYCLE

Why is it that love
Resplendent in all its grandeur
Has such a long dark shadow
Called pain ?

Why is it that those you care about
Can hurt you deeply ?
Undoubtedly ?
As I gaze upon the face of love
And feel it wrap me with warm gloves
As I snuggle down in love's arms

As I am lured
To let my guard down
And feel more secure
I feel a sharp stabbing pain
The sun of life has moved along its path
And love casts its shadow over me

Oh the shivers and the chills
The ever deepening darkness
The sadness
The despair

But I know
That life's sun follows a path
It rises and sets only to rise again
And the cycle repeats itself

My pain is temporary
The despair will pass
As surely as I know
That there will be sunrise
The shadow shall recede
Once again behind love's regal back
And I shall once again
Be ensconced in the
Warm embrace of love

© Toki Mabogunje
1998

TUNNEL OF BABEL
Or
BABEL IN THE SUBWAY

It slithers into its tunnel hole
That modern silver metal worm
To make one of several stops
On route to its ultimate destination
To regurgitate or ingest
The mass of humanity
Anxious to be carried
Within its belly
From one place to the next

The silver coloured plate doors
Slide open and shut
Regurgitating first then ingesting
Before moving noisily
Into the mysterious beyond

I sit and I watch
The flurry of activity
At this particular stop

Toki & Damola Mabogunje

People rushing back and forth
The homeless sleeping
On wooden benches
Musicians playing
To the delight of commuters who strain
To hear the music

The sound of screeching brakes
And clacking of wheels on rails
These great silver earthworms
Pull in and leave the stop
The babble of human voices
The clatter of human feet
Creates such a cacophony of sound
Could it have been this bad
In the tower of Babel ?

© Toki Mabogunje
1999 New York City Subway

LIFE'S JOURNEY

This life's journey
Is ever so interesting
With its twists and turns
Its ups and downs
Always revealing
Something new

We begin our journey
Our parents and society
Providing the tools
We need to be
Cartographers

We draw our maps
Believing we know
Exactly where we are going
As if in response to this
Life brings us unexpectedly
Upon new uncharted territory

We feel almost like we
Need to begin again
What is this place?
Unknown to us
We look for a way around it
And find the wonder of nature
That there's no other way
But to go through it

Toki & Damola Mabogunje

As we journey
This uncharted territory
We discover we already have
The tools we need
But learn new ways
To utilize these tools
To find our way
We learn the lessons
We need to learn
And suddenly we are
Back on track

The key we discover
Much later in life
Is to journey as if anew
To embrace each situation we encounter
With the freshness and newness of life
To live ever in the present
Not in the past or in the future
To realize that life
Is the greatest gift of all

© Toki Mabogunje
June 22nd 1999
New York City

THE GAME MACHINE

I feel like I am looking at a chess board
You make your move
And I make mine
We both know what the odds may be

It is interesting this game we play
Sometimes relaxing
At other times exciting

Chances are that life is
Not about what we do
Or where we end up
It's about ....
The interplay betwixt and between
The other players on the board
The things that happen despite us
It's not a chessboard is it ?
It's a gaming machine
A lot more is left to chance

Sit back and watch
Detach yourself
And admire the kaleidoscope before you
Revel in it like a child
Without a care in the world

Let's play together
You and I
This game machine of life

© Toki Mabogunje
November 25th 1999
Lagos

ONE FINE DAY

One fine day
Just as I anticipated
He walked in
Tall, dark and gay

That rush of feeling
Suddenly nervous
Suddenly anxious
Wondering, smiling
Thinking why me ?

A stolen kiss
A warm embrace
Stolen moments
Precious bliss

An open conversation
Totally trusting
Blindly accepting
No nuances
No misgivings
Just the realization

That this moment in time
Engraved in your memory
With our unspoken desires
Shall one fine day
Be mine

© Toki Mabogunje
April 6th 2000

DESPAIR

When all your troubles
Overwhelm you
And you feel helpless
And adrift

When all your sorrows
Envelope you
And you feel lost
In the darkness of it

When all despair
Grabs at your heart
And gives it
A painful tug

Where can you go
To seek solace
And a warm and loving hug

© Toki Mabogunje
July 10th 2000
Lagos

Toki & Damola Mabogunje

CHILDREN AT PLAY

Look at them
Come and play
Look at them
Children I say

Light of life
Life of light
Hurrah Hurrah
Children at flight

They laugh
They clap
They sing
They dance

They fight
They hurt
They want more
Than just turf

Children at play
What can I say
Free and wild
No restrictions, no inhibitions
Just fun, just child

You free my spirit
You loosen my smile
I feel the wonder
I feel it child

© Toki Mabogunje
April 24th 2000
Easter, Ijebu

DESIRE

It is not going to happen is it ?
The fulfillment of this desire
This connection soul to soul
Mind to mind

It is such a pity
Because I have so much to give
And so much I want
In return

My dream has turned into a mirage
No longer an aim, goal or vision
To strive for and attain
But something that is not real
Something that appears and disappears at will
And seems not to have substance

Maybe my desire is so strong
I refuse to see the writing on the wall
Maybe I am so thick
I do not understand simple language
But one thing I know for sure
There are few things I have wanted so badly

Here I am trying so hard to get away from pain
To experience pure joy
Even if for a short while
Only to find the path so rough and thorny
Such a difficult terrain
Makes my vision hard to attain

I am lost you know
Lost in a maze of wanna bes
And wanna haves
If the situation were not so heart rending
I would want to laugh

But I can't
My trembling lips
My blurred vision
My bleeding heart and soul
Are such a sorry sight

© Toki Mabogunje
November 2000 Lagos

COOKIES AND CREAM

Oh! Sweet Dreams
Of cookies and cream
Oreos, chocolate and dark
With frothy white cream
Sandwiched in between

Rivulets of sinful thought
Desire strong and taut
Coursing through my veins
One thought like a teardrop
Rolls into another
Oh! The tingles, the passion
Difficult to smother

Pleasure wraps softly around me
As light brown lips glisten
Moist with anticipation
Open up to envelope
The very tip of temptation

Soft lips move ever so gently
Sucking, releasing, up and down
Eyes closed expectant
As the sweet frothy liquid
Reaches the crown

Savour and taste it
Vanilla with a hint of
Cinnamon and Mint
Thick, velvety, smooth
Will it satisfy? Will it sooth?

Can't tarry
Must hurry
More frantic
In a state of panic

Ah! At last it's done
The milk shake is all gone
The experience is bitter sweet
The event is incomplete

Didn't get the Oreos
Nor the cookies and cream
Didn't get the chocolate
With the velvet white cream
Sandwiched in between

© Toki Mabogunje
5th November 2002

SILENCE

What is this silence?
So loud and deafening
It is scary
Like standing on the edge
Of a precipice
Should I jump and let it
Envelope me
Or do I step back into
The maddening noise
Of every day living

What is this silence?
I shout and all I get
Is my echo
There is no response
Where are you?
Where is my life-line
To sanity ?
Where is my connection
To experiencing that which
Is outside the noise and
Mayhem behind me ?

Dare I open my eyes ?
What might I find ?
A black hole ?
A steep incline ?
Am I in the wilderness ?
I may be on a mountain top
Or I may be alone ?

Shall I reach out ?
And hope that you are there
Silently watching me
Fighting the same fears,
Hopes, dreams and desires

Will you reach out to me ?
What is this silence ?
Answer me !!

© Toki Mabogunje
6pm J.B. OYE'S HOUSE
IBADAN
December 31st 2002

The Duet An Anthology of Poems

DIVINE MOMENTS

I relive those moments in Calabar
Play them over, my mind ajar
The serenity of the place
Being one with the human race

I am grateful to coincidence
The great creator of possibilities
The opportunity given to attend
The gift of providence

Why did you heed the call ?
What have you fulfilled after all ?
Has a fruitful seed been planted
Or were you just having fun?

The fusion of mind and body
The molding of desires divine
Wrapped with warm and loving assistance
Let's give up our age old resistance

Oh what divine moments
Such a pleasure to recall and more
Remain not just a memory
Let's repeat it. Encore! Encore!

© Toki Mabogunje
July 18th 2004

CRUSHED

There I am on the soft dewy forest floor
In all my morning glory
Fragile, exposed. A fresh allure

Then you come racing
Through the underbrush
Seemingly uncaring
Bent on your mission
In the lushness of the bush

I get trampled
I get crushed
My unspoken feelings hushed

If only you knew
How much it hurt
If you could hear
My heart blurt

If only you could feel
My soul crumble
The depths of pain
Makes one humble

My love and hope thrashed
While you go the distance
Not once looking back
At the damage in this instance

It all seems so meaningless
So hopeless now
Why open up in the morning
To receive the morning dew
Why turn my face up
To feel the sunlight anew

I droop and fold my petals
Wrap them around my
Wounded feelings
Protection for my survival
In all my future dealings

© Toki Mabogunje
August 2nd 2004

BREATHLESS

Tall and Regal
A furrow on his brow
Puzzled, always puzzled
At little vagaries
The happenings in life's flow

Rushing, always rushing
Jacket flapping in the wind
Briefcase held tightly in his hands
Tied directly to his heart string

Serious, always serious
Ideas and thoughts sublime
Articulate but much too detailed
Could make me delirious, so delirious

A sense of humour?
Yes sometimes
Sometimes I laugh
It's not a rumour
Ah ha ha ha

Pleasant but full of feeling
Dutiful, yet he is bleeding
Catch your breath
Don't cock your head
Breathe, keep breathing

© Toki Mabogunje
4th November 2004
Written for my friend Soboma

IMAGES

Tall, dark and willowy
With a beautiful bright white smile
How can we add substance
To your presence

How do I make you real
How do I cramp your style
Here! Yet not there
Wispy and ephemeral
Reach out to the shadowy presence
Reach out and fall

Don't disappear
Please don't
Your presence is comforting
Come to life, once in awhile
Come to life
So your loving can be felt

Don't grasp, don't grab
Be gentle, touch softly
Sh sh sh whisper don't talk
Stay ……. Task gently

© Toki Mabogunje
October 2004

Toki & Damola Mabogunje

WHAT IS WROOONG WITH YOU!?

So I went to the station the other day
To wait for the next train coming my way
Then I notice this white lady staring at me
But I dismiss it casually

So I take a seat on the bench that she's sitting on
She not only gravitates but she gets up from
The bench as she moves to the other side
Now that just pisses me off

So because I'm black I'm not human too?
Just 'cuz I'm black, I can't sit beside you?
Because I'm black you need to be careful? fearful? Now
you're gonna get an earful.
See Lady, What is WroOong with YOU!?

I thought racism was dead in philly...
Before I met you.
I thought opinions

were changing too...
Before I met you.

I might have understood if it was a dark alleyway,
A passage, secluded, so late in the day
But at a train station to a student like me!?
Gosh Lady, What is WroOong with You!!!

It is now the year 2006
It no longer matters if you're black or mixed
Or yellow or purple or any color
All humans are equal, none is superior

So its time for you to reevaluate
That outdated, archaic, system of hate
That stupid and ancient fear of all colors dark
Because one day, I won't just pass the remark

What is WroOong with YOU!!!?

Because one day it'll be a matter of fact
There IS something wrong with you

Because one day, when you choose to act like that
The victim WILL tell you that he's pissed
And unlike me, HE'LL do it with his Fists

Because Lady,
YOU, are wrong in what you do.

©Damola Mabogunje
Saturday, October 14, 2006

Toki & Damola Mabogunje

THE VALUE OF A LIFE

With all the guns, drugs and Violence today
The value of a life seems to have decayed
Depreciated, belittled and deprecated
The value of a life, needs to be re-evaluated

The value of a life is the labor of birth
The value of a life is your trials at work
The value of a life is the way you feel
When you wake up to a steaming hot bowl of cereal

The value of a life is your very first kiss
The value of a life is your child's first step
The value of a life is even more than this
The value of a life is your very first breadth

The value of a life is that Christmas morning
When you woke up to find all that you wanted
The value of a life is that New Year's Eve
When the fireworks were too amazing to believe

The value of a life is that dream where you can fly
The one where you're in love and the one where you're at war
The value of a life is the girl that got away,
The drink you never had and the sight you never saw

The value of a life is the person next door
Who plays his music loud and throws parties every night
The value of a life is the person upstairs
Who last Halloween, gave you such a fright

The value of a life is your husband who snores
Your son who never does his chores
"The nagging wife."

The value of a life is your wedding day
Your vacation stay
Your honeymoon at the bay

The value of a life is when you broke that leg
That took 2 months to heal on its own
How everyone signed on your cast
And how no one left you alone

The value of a life is when you were sick in bed
Your kids cooked for you
Your loved one stayed home

The value of a life is your first boyfriend
First break-up
And first make-up

The value of a life is your uncle George
Your cousin Annabelle
Your Grand-ma Marge

The value of life is all your hopes and dreams
The things you've done and all you have seen
Your character flaws and your character boons
Your varied opinions and differing moods

Life is all you are
And all you can be
This is what life means to me

And although life is fleeting and transient by nature
And the boom of a gun could mean a life is gone
The value of life is astounding you see
Because life itself is priceless to me.

©Damola Mabogunje
1/28/2006 2:54p.m

MERCY, WHY DO YOU SPARE ME?

Mercy, its 4a.m
And I have a question for you
Why do you spare me the punishment
When you know the sins that I do?

Why do you still shine the light
When my mind is full of temptation
As I neither act nor do right?

Are you patronizing me?
Or just watching me punish myself
Guilt ridden, my conscience nags me

Mercy why is it that no matter what
You never forsake me?
Even when my back is turned
Beside me I still see

You trying to help me turn about
And correct my ways
Still giving me some kind of grace
Still showing me your smiling face

Mercy, you know its kinda sad
Self-pity is depressing
And you know what makes me mad?
Its that I still have your blessing

(sobbing)
Mercy, why don't you punish me?
Make me do your bidding
Why don't you be more than a guide
Be my direct path

Mercy, why do you spare me?
When you see the way I am
Mercy I swear it was not my fault (crying)
When I stole your pounded-yam....

©Damola Mabogunje
Wednesday, September 13, 2006.

www.ingramcontent.com/pod-product-compliance
Lightning Source LLC
Chambersburg PA
CBHW032016290426
44109CB00013B/684